Climate Change

Written by Hannah Reed

Explorations

Contents

Our changing climate

Earth's **climate** is always changing. This has been the case for millions and millions of years. There have been cooler periods called ice ages, followed by periods when the earth's climate has become warmer. Fifteen thousand years ago the Sahara Desert was covered in grass. In the last ice age about 10,000 years ago most of North America was covered in a sheet of ice more than one mile (1.6 kilometers) thick.

In the last 100 years, the earth's average temperature has risen. **Global warming** is the term used to describe this increase in the earth's temperature. This doesn't mean that we never have any cold days or that every day will be very hot. It simply means that each year the average temperature on Earth is increasing.

Scientists have recorded that:

- the average temperature of the land on Earth has increased

- the average temperature of the ocean has also increased

- there is now less land covered by ice and snow than there was 100 years ago

- the average sea level has risen.

How will these changes affect the environment and the earth's climate? Will the changes affect the way we live on Earth and the things that we do?

Earth's climate

What is climate?

Climate describes the weather conditions of a particular place measured over many years. It describes the average temperature, amount of sunshine, cloud cover, and rain or snow that falls each year.

Do different places have different climates?

Yes. Some places on Earth are hotter than others because they receive different amounts of the sun's heat. The equator is closer to the sun so places at the equator are hot. The North Pole and South Pole are further from the sun so the climate is colder.   Conditions in the **atmosphere** such as cloud cover and wind affect the climate of a place.

What is the atmosphere?

The atmosphere is the layer of gases that surround Earth. This is where all weather happens. The atmosphere contains the oxygen that we need to breathe, it protects us from the sun's radiation, and it keeps Earth warm. Without the atmosphere, there would be no life on Earth.

How does the atmosphere help to keep the earth warm?

The gases in the atmosphere trap some of the sun's heat and prevent it from escaping into space. These gases are called **greenhouse gases** because they trap the sun's heat in the same way as glass in a greenhouse does.

A greenhouse is made of glass. It lets in the sun's light and heat. When it cools down outside, the heat inside the greenhouse is trapped by the glass and the greenhouse stays warm. Without the greenhouse gases in the atmosphere, the temperature of Earth would be well below freezing.

Greenhouse gases

Greenhouse gases are:

carbon dioxide

water vapor

methane

nitrous oxide.

▼ The greenhouse effect

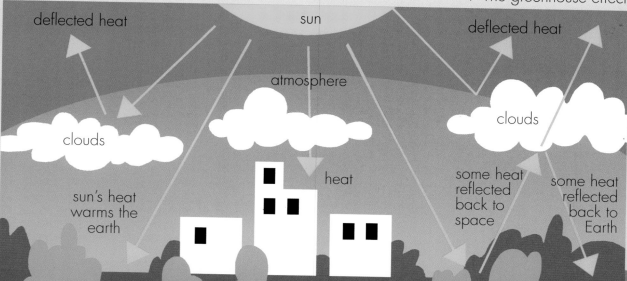

deflected heat

sun

deflected heat

atmosphere

clouds

clouds

heat

sun's heat warms the earth

some heat reflected back to space

some heat reflected back to Earth

Why are more greenhouse gases being released into the atmosphere?

Over the last 100 years the amount of greenhouse gases in the atmosphere has increased. The greenhouse gas **carbon dioxide** is produced when we use fuels such as oil, gas, or coal. These fuels are called **fossil fuels** because they were made from the remains of plants and animals which formed fossils thousands of years ago.

Most industries use fossil fuels to power the machines that produce the things that we use every day. When these fuels are burned they release the greenhouse gas carbon dioxide into the atmosphere. Whenever we heat or cool our homes, cook meals, or use vehicles powered by oil or gas, carbon dioxide is released into the atmosphere.

As well as putting more carbon dioxide into the atmosphere, less carbon dioxide is being taken out by trees and plants. This is because people have cleared forests and wetlands.

As the level of greenhouse gases in the atmosphere increases, the **greenhouse effect** also increases. These gases are building up like a heavy blanket surrounding the earth and trapping heat.

This graph shows that as the amount of gases released by industry has increased, there has been an increase in the level of greenhouse gases in the atmosphere.

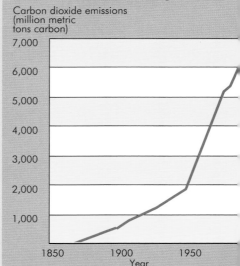

Increase in the level of greenhouse gases as a result of industry

Carbon dioxide emissions (million metric tons carbon)

7,000	
6,000	
5,000	
4,000	
3,000	
2,000	
1,000	

1850   1900   1950

Year

Carbon dioxide facts

- About 75 percent of carbon dioxide people have put into the atmosphere comes from burning fossil fuels such as coal, oil, and natural gas.

- About 25 percent of the carbon dioxide people are responsible for is the result of changed land use, especially deforestation.

- The amount of carbon dioxide in the atmosphere has increased by 31 percent since 1750.

- The present level of carbon dioxide in the atmosphere is higher than at any time in the past 420,000 years and is possibly higher than any time in the last 20 million years.

The carbon cycle

Carbon is a substance that is found in living things, such as plants and animals, as well as some non-living things such as rocks and soil. Carbon dioxide is a gas. It is a mixture of carbon and oxygen. It is the most important greenhouse gas.

Carbon constantly moves in a cycle between the atmosphere and Earth's surface. For thousands of years, the amount of carbon released in the atmosphere has been about the same as the amount taken out of the atmosphere.

In the last 100 years, human activities, such as burning fossil fuels, have put more carbon dioxide into the atmosphere than has been removed. Cutting down forests has meant that less carbon is removed from the atmosphere – trees take in carbon dioxide from the air to make food. The carbon cycle is no longer in balance.

1. Plants use carbon dioxide from soil and the air to make food. This is called photosynthesis.
2. When animals or plants die, the carbon goes back into the soil.
3. When animals eat plants, they use the carbon in plants to grow. When animals breathe out they put carbon dioxide back into the air.
4. When trees are destroyed, they no longer use carbon dioxide from the atmosphere, so there is a higher level in the air.
5. Smoke from forest fires is full of carbon.
6. Oil, gas, and coal are mined from deep in the ground. When these fuels are burned, carbon is released into the atmosphere.
7. Carbon moves between the ocean and atmosphere.

The carbon cycle

Offshore oil rig

Carbon

Carbon is found in many things on Earth:

rocks and soil	coal	plants
sea water	diamonds	oil
animals	charcoal	gas

Did you know?

In 2005, about 7.9 billion tons of carbon were released globally. This is an increase of 2.5 percent each year since 2000.

How do we know it's getting warmer?

In the last 100 years, the part of the **atmosphere** closest to Earth as well as the upper part of the ocean have warmed. The rise in temperature varies in different parts of the world, with the temperatures at the North Pole and South Pole rising the most.

Changes in average temperature

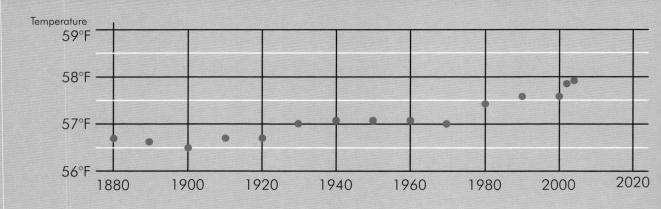

Scientists collect, measure, and study information so they can understand how the rise in the earth's temperature will affect the **climate**.

Climate change is the term used to describe what happens when the earth's climate changes over a long time.

Scientists in Antarctica drill deep into the ice to collect ice samples.

Looking in the ice

Scientists study samples of ice to find out about the earth's past climate. They drill more than 1 mile (1.6 kilometers) down into the ice in Antarctica to collect ice samples. As they drill deeper, they reach older ice. This enables scientists to study ice that is hundreds of thousands of years old.

Air bubbles trapped in ice contain gases which were in the atmosphere when the ice was formed. Scientists measure the amounts of gases trapped in air bubbles in the ice. By doing this, scientists have found that there is more **carbon dioxide** in the air today than there was hundreds of thousands of years ago.

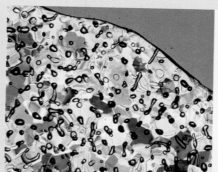

A sliver of Antarctic ice. Tiny, trapped air bubbles are shown in color.

Tracking changes to the earth's climate

1950s

1950s: Scientists all around the world begin collecting data on carbon dioxide levels in the atmosphere.

1970s

1970s: Scientists collect and test stored air samples from Antarctica. They detect an increase in carbon levels. At the same time they record an increase in world temperatures. This leads to scientists talking about an increase in the **greenhouse effect**. Some scientists disagree, claiming that there have always been changes in world temperatures.

1980s

1980s: Scientists start taking samples from the ice sheets in Greenland and Antarctica. By looking at how this ice has formed, scientists have been able to measure temperature change in these places over the last 100,000 years. They found that since the 1950s the rate of warming has increased rapidly.

1988

1988: The **United Nations** form a group of the world's best scientists to study the latest scientific information on **global warming**. This group is called the Intergovernmental Panel on Climate Change (IPCC). They report on the increase in **greenhouse gases** and their effect on climate.

Findings from the IPCC report, 2007

- The average land temperature on Earth has increased by 1.4 degrees Fahrenheit (0.76 degrees Celsius) over the last 100 years.

- The average temperature of the ocean has also increased.

- There is now less land covered by ice and snow than there was 100 years ago.

- The average sea level has risen.

Did you know?

The IPCC is made up of more than 2,500 scientists from 130 countries.

4 Global warming and the environment

There are likely to be many changes to the environment as a result of **global warming**. **Glaciers**, **ice caps**, and sea ice will probably melt faster than they usually would. Sea levels are expected to rise, and oceans may become warmer. Heavier rainfall is likely to occur in some places, while other areas will receive less than expected. Changes such as these could greatly affect animals that live in these environments. This may lead to many animals becoming **endangered** or **extinct**.

Did you know?

It is predicted that many plant and animal **species** may become extinct as the earth's **climate** warms and their **habitats** change.

1967

2007

▲ These Greenpeace images show how part of the Halong glacier in Mt. Everest has retreated over 40 years.

Glaciers and ice caps

In the Arctic region, the temperatures are rising faster than elsewhere. At the same time, the Arctic ice cap has decreased in size. Since 1978, the Arctic sea ice has shrunk by 2.7 percent every 10 years.

Many glaciers on Earth are melting. Glaciers are rivers of ice. They form when the snow that doesn't melt each year is compacted into ice that slowly moves down hills and mountains. Each year, the edge of a glacier shrinks and expands depending on how much ice melts in summer and how much snow falls in winter. Since 1985, however, most of the world's glaciers have been **retreating**.

People whose water supply comes from melting snow and ice will be greatly affected if glaciers and ice caps disappear.

Glacier National Park

Glacier National Park in the Rocky Mountains, USA, is famous for its glaciers. But these glaciers have been rapidly melting since the park opened in 1910. Scientists have recorded significant changes in the climate in the area, including an increase in the daily minimum temperatures. Scientists have predicted that all of the park's glaciers may disappear by 2030.

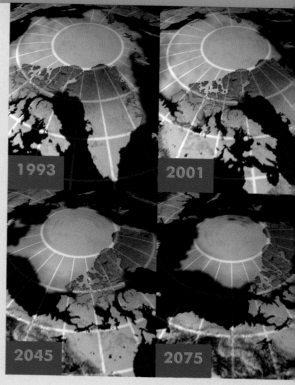

1993   2001   2045   2075

▲ Scientists predict that the Arctic ice cap will shrink if temperatures continue to rise.

Warmer oceans

Ocean waters are warmed by the sun. As the earth's temperature warms up so too does the ocean's temperature. Ocean temperatures vary from place to place. They are warmest near the equator and coldest near the Arctic and Antarctic circles. The deeper the ocean water, the colder it is. Changes in ocean temperatures affect the plants and animals that live there. Over the last 50 years scientists have found that the overall temperature of the world's oceans has increased.

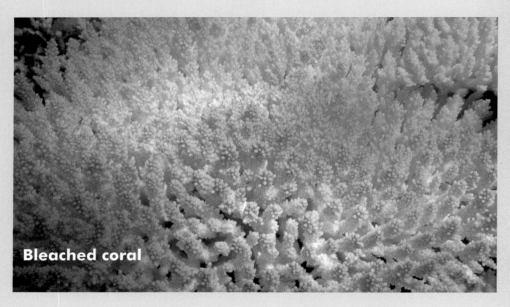

Bleached coral

Bleaching coral reefs

Coral reefs provide a home for many of the world's fish. When the water gets too warm, corals lose their bright colors and become white. This is called coral bleaching. If the warmer water is only temporary then the coral can recover. If not, the coral can die. Also, if the sea water becomes too warm, it may kill the coral **polyps**.

Great Barrier Reef

The Great Barrier Reef stretches more than 1,600 miles (2,300 kilometers) along the east coast of Australia. It is made up of more than 2,900 individual coral reefs and is the world's largest coral reef system. Over the last 10 years, almost one-fifth of this reef has been affected by coral bleaching.

In 1998, 16 percent of the reef was destroyed as a result of coral bleaching. This coincided with coral bleaching in many other parts of the world. In 2002 and 2006, more coral was damaged. Scientists believe that climate change may be responsible for some or all of these bleaching events.

Great Barrier Reef

Australia

◄ After heavy rains, flooding causes havoc in the low-lying land in Bangladesh.

Rising sea levels

If the earth's temperature continues to increase, sea levels are highly likely to rise. This is because of melting sea ice and warming ocean waters. When the earth's sheet ice melts, the water runs into the sea. As the ocean's waters become warmer they expand and take up more space. In the last 100 years, the sea level has risen 4 inches (10 centimeters) in some places, and up to 10 inches (25 centimeters) in others.

When an area is flooded, people's homes are washed away, leaving many people homeless. People are more likely to become ill as diseases spread more easily in water.

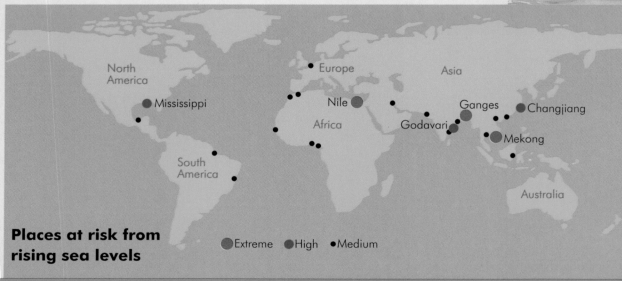

North America

Europe

Asia

Mississippi

Nile

Ganges

Changjiang

Africa

Godavari

South America

Mekong

Australia

Places at risk from rising sea levels

⬤ Extreme ⬤ High • Medium

Greenland

Greenland is an island near the Arctic Circle. It is mostly covered with an enormous sheet of ice that is over 1 mile (1.6 kilometers) thick. Each year scientists measure how much of the ice sheet melts over the summer. They also measure how much ice re-forms during the winter as snow falls on the ice sheet.

Scientists studying this ice sheet observed that over the last five years the edge of the ice sheet has melted at a faster rate than before. If the ice sheet continues to melt at this rate, a huge amount of fresh water will be released into the ocean. This would lead to a significant rise in sea levels.

▼ The Greenland ice sheet

Changing weather patterns

Over the last 100 years, the average temperature on Earth has increased. In the last 50 years there have been fewer cold days, cold nights, and frosts. At the same time, hot days and hot nights have become more frequent. It seems most likely that this trend will continue.

Scientists from the IPCC have predicted the weather changes that seem most likely, and how these changes will affect farming, water supplies, and how we live.

Likely change in weather	Over most land areas, fewer cold days and nights; warmer and more frequent hot days and nights
Effect on farming	Colder areas will have a longer growing season Warmer areas will have a shorter growing season due to droughts
Effect on water supply	Areas that rely on melting snow for water will be affected
Effect on how we live	Fewer people will suffer from **exposure** to freezing cold weather

Did you know?

Severe, long droughts have been recorded in places such as Africa and Australia since 2000. These have had a devastating effect on farmers and other people who depend on growing food to make their living.

Heat waves	Some places will receive more rain, and bigger and more frequent floods	Some places will receive less rain and areas affected by drought will increase	More intense **cyclones** and more cyclones overall
Less farming in warm areas due to increased heat Increased danger of wildfires	Heavy downpours of rain can damage crops, wash away soil, and make the soil waterlogged	Less water will be available for people to use in their homes, and in farming and industry	Cyclones can damage crops and uproot trees
Greater demand on water supplies	Quality of water can be reduced by flooding Spread of diseases in water Increased water supply in some places	Reduced water supply	Water supply can be stopped due to power failures
Greater risk of people suffering from heat-related illnesses	Loss of houses and buildings from floods Disruption of everyday activities due to flooding	Risk of reduced food and water	Floods and high winds can injure or kill people and destroy the places where they live

What can be done?

People around the world are looking at ways to reduce **global warming**. Everyone can help including your government, your community, and your family. There are many ways that we can reduce the amount of **carbon dioxide** (also known as CO_2) we release into the **atmosphere**.

Kyoto Protocol

The Kyoto Protocol is an international agreement. Its aim is to get countries to reduce their **greenhouse gas** emissions. Many countries have passed laws to force industries to reduce the amount of carbon they release into the atmosphere. But not all countries have signed the agreement.

▲ The Gherkin in London is a modern building that was designed with a natural air ventilation system. It uses half the power that a similar sized office tower would use.

Using non-motorized transportation such as cycling does not release CO_2

Improved farming methods can help reduce CO_2 in the atmosphere

Using solar power does not release CO_2 into the atmosphere

Governments and business

Governments can make laws that limit the amount of carbon dioxide that factories and other **industries** release into the atmosphere. They can also give industries money for research. This helps them to find cleaner ways to make the products we use every day. It also helps them to make products that produce less carbon dioxide.

Governments have also spent a lot of money on advertising programs that show people how they can reduce their impact on the climate. These programs teach us about what the problem is and what we can do to help solve it. Governments also help people to use alternative forms of power. They can do this by refunding some of the money people spend when they choose cleaner forms of **energy**.

Governments can make laws that enable us to make changes to:

- energy supply
- transportation
- buildings
- industry
- agriculture
- forestry waste

▲ A **geothermal** power station, an alternative energy source

Alternative sources of energy

People are developing alternative ways of making electricity to reduce the use of **fossil fuels**. These include using solar energy, wind energy, water energy, tidal energy, geothermal energy, and nuclear energy.

Solar power

Electricity can be made by using the sun's energy. Solar panels collect the sun's energy and change it into electricity that can be used to power electrical devices. This form of electricity is called clean energy because it does not release carbon dioxide into the atmosphere.

▲ Hydroelectric project, James Bay, Canada

▼ The sun's energy can be harnessed to produce solar power.

▼ Solar panels

Wind power

Wind power is where huge windmills are turned by the wind to make electricity. Around the world, power companies are building wind farms to generate electricity. This is also a clean form of energy.

Water power

In mountainous areas, fast-flowing water is used to generate electricity. This is called hydroelectricity.

Water is also used in this way in tidal power stations where the movement of waves, as the tides come in and go out, is used to generate electricity.

Geothermal power stations also use steam that is trapped underground to generate electricity.

What can be done?

Reducing our carbon footprint

We all use things that put carbon into the air. The amount of carbon we put into the air is called our carbon footprint. The size of our carbon footprint depends on the choices we make and how we live our lives. Here are some ways you can reduce your carbon footprint.

◄ When you walk or ride a bike instead of traveling in a car you are helping to reduce the amount of carbon released into the atmosphere.

Action to reduce the amount of carbon dioxide being released into the atmosphere	Replace regular light bulbs with compact fluorescent bulbs	When it is cold, put on a sweater and turn the heat down to 64° Fahrenheit (18° Celsius). When it is hot, turn the air conditioner up to 72° Fahrenheit (22° Celsius). Only run the air conditioner when it is very hot	Ask your parents to set the hot water heater to 120° Fahrenheit (49° Celsius). 	Take short showers (3 minutes) Ask your parents to replace your shower head with a low flow one 
Amount saved	100 pounds (45 kilograms) per year	up to 2,000 pounds (907 kilograms) per year	up to 500 pounds (227 kilograms) per year	up to 650 pounds (295 kilograms) per year

Did you know?

Carbon dioxide stays in the atmosphere for a long time. More than half of the carbon dioxide released by burning fossil fuels in the last 100 years is still in the atmosphere.

► Try planting a tree. A fully grown tree can take as much as 200 pounds (91 kilograms) of carbon a year out of the atmosphere.

Buy things that have the smallest amount of packaging to reduce the amount of garbage you produce	Recycle or reuse as many things as you can	Unplug electrical appliances when they are not in use	Only run the dishwasher when it is full	Use a push mower instead of a gasoline-powered or electric mower	Hang your clothes on a clothesline outside rather than use a dryer
up to 1,200 pounds (540 kilograms) per year	up to 1,000 pounds (454 kilograms) per year	up to 1,000 pounds (454 kilograms) per year	up to 200 pounds (91 kilograms) per year	80 pounds a year (36 kilograms) (and you get fit)	up to 700 pounds (318 kilograms) per year

Conclusion

Global warming and climate change are likely to remain one of the biggest challenges of the 21st century.

No one can say what the future will be like for the earth's climate. Scientists can measure changes and predict trends, but they cannot be certain what the weather and climate will be like in the future.

And every day we can help reduce global warming by reducing the amount of carbon we release into the air.

Glossary

atmosphere   the air made up of gases that surround the earth

carbon dioxide   a greenhouse gas that forms when fossil fuels are used

climate   the overall weather conditions of a region

cyclone   a tropical storm of winds at least 39 miles (63 kilometers) per hour

endangered   at great risk of becoming extinct

energy   what is used to power machines

exposure   left open to nature's extremes, such as sun, wind, rain, etc.

extinct   no longer exists, usually applies to a plant or animal species

fossil fuels   fuels such as oil, gas, or coal, which are made from the remains of ancient plant and animal fossils in the earth

geothermal   heat produced naturally underground

glaciers   rivers of ice

global warming   increase of the earth's average temperature over several years

greenhouse effect   the increased warming of the earth by trapping the sun's heat

greenhouse gases   gases in the earth's atmosphere that trap the sun's heat

habitats   places where a plant or an animal naturally lives

ice caps   ice masses that cover less than 31,000 square miles (50,000 square kilometers)

industries   groups of businesses that make a certain item, e.g. the car industry

polyps   small animals with a fixed base, tentacles, and a mouth, such as coral

retreating   shrinking

species   a group of living things that are able to reproduce with each other

United Nations   international organization of governments working together to promote and protect peace, security, and human rights around the world

Index